Louis-Philippe Hébert

MISTER BLACKHURST

Translated by Ardeth Neale

BookLand press

Published by BookLand Press
15 Allstate Parkway, Suite 600, Markham, Ontario L3R 5B4
www.booklandpress.com

Printed in Canada

Front cover image © Edsaez

Library and Archives Canada Cataloguing in Publication

Hébert, Louis-Philippe, 1946-
[Monsieur Blacquières. English]
Mister Blackhurst / Louis-Philippe Hébert; translated by Ardeth Neale.

Translation of: Monsieur Blacquières.
Poems.
Issued in print and electronic formats.
ISBN 978-1-77231-056-6 (softcover).--ISBN 978-1-77231-057-3 (EPUB).--ISBN 978-1-77231-058-0 (PDF)

I. Neale, Ardeth, translator II. Title. III. Title: Mister Blackhurst. IV. Title: Monsieur Blacquières. English.

PS8515.E2M6713 2018 C841'.54 C2017-907132-7
C2017-907133-5

Canada Council for the Arts | Conseil des arts du Canada

ONTARIO ARTS COUNCIL
CONSEIL DES ARTS DE L'ONTARIO
an Ontario government agency
un organisme du gouvernement de l'Ontario

We acknowledge the financial support of the Government of Canada through the National Translation Program for Book Publishing, an initiative of the *Roadmap for Canada's Official Languages 2013-2018: Education, Immigration, Communities*, for our translation activities. We acknowledge the support of the Canada Council for the Arts, which last year invested $153 million to bring the arts to Canadians throughout the country. We acknowledge the support of the Ontario Arts Council (OAC), an agency of the Government of Ontario.

A trace left behind is a stain that remains

there is nothing here
not a table
not even a bed
one day they came
one day, like yesterday
or this morning
or during the night
they took everything away

they said:
you won't need these anymore
they scooped it all up
all that was lying around
all that was not
they put everything into the boxes
they had brought

they were good boxes
that much I'll say!
boxes that had never been used
none of that sticky tape, yellow
and brittle
that shreds as you try to tear it off
the corners of the boxes were perfectly square
their walls were intact
along the sides, there were no traces left
from Exacto knives
the bottoms were unwarped
these were indeed good boxes
really, I am telling you

boxes
unbruised, free of those cuts
that for humans and other animals
would become wounds and infections

no detail escaped my notice
the manufacturer's name in blue
the orange logo made up of two triangles, right-angled
        with a space wedged between the two hypotenuses
now here was something the poet mathematician Al-Kashi
        would have liked
you see, I too have a knack for detail

and besides, it had *Budget* printed in large letters
    as if to caution
that when you get the notion to leave
there is always a price to pay

the empty space between the triangles represents
    an invisible road
an optical illusion created by the angle
    separating the two hypotenuses
which appear destined to meet at infinity
since the triangle above is more tapered
    than the one below

I must admit, I would have preferred isosceles triangles
the boxes, for their part, were perfectly symmetric
perfect symmetry is possible
it is how a cube is best defined
the flaps were fitted
the fluted cardboard
corrugated
had not been subject to moisture
there was nothing hand-written
nothing crossed out
no needless words

impeccable boxes
which I much appreciated
I saw it as a sign of courtesy
toward me
a mark of consideration
they had chosen brand new boxes
from the warehouse
boxes that had never been used
and all that for me
can you believe it?
the effort
the selection
the expense

I was grateful
I don't know why
old boxes
their corners crushed
the sides slashed
sinister
like cheeks scarred
flanks covered in wounds
sutures held together by tape
          reinforced with nylon threads
boxes tattooed with words
recklessly inscribed
like on the arms of roustabouts
would have made me feel less considered

I know that it is silly on my part
you can get too wrapped up in details in the end
I have no doubt that it matters none
to those two men in suits
no more than
the colour of their shoes
which were black, I had noted
no more important
than the nets over their hair
even though one had a shaved head
with only a soft black fuzz
on the surface of his scalp

they were most kind
and I'm not talking about roustabouts
as you might have guessed

it is a precious thing, kindness
we never appreciate it enough
in this case, it was expressed by new boxes
I could have commended them
although I didn't
I am not trying to flatter anyone
by saying so
but boxes are important
to me, for me
always for me
even though they don't have the same significance

for others, I will grant you that
or at least, not everyone
I'm thinking only of myself
that's how I am
I have already been reproached for that, by a woman

a box is inviting
I know that cats go in boxes
kittens
you can add a blanket
if you wish
it's the mother who likes that
the mother cat
the smell of the cardboard
more likely the smell of glue
actually
its odours intermingle with those of the blanket
you should never use a new blanket
for that very reason
kittens, cats ready to give birth
to drop, can you say that
for cats
to drop
an old blanket
that's what you're supposed to use
impregnated with smells
I'm not saying that birthing stinks
but death, now that stinks

there is glue, it's true
and, in glue, there is an odour of vinegar
between face A and face B
when you put your nose up to it
you can see, between the two faces, a wavy sheet
a sheet of thick paper
not the type on which you would write
stories or poetry
not paper of the hygienic sort either
Kraft paper, that's it
for it to keep its shape, it takes glue
to maintain the waviness
like waves on the ocean
ah, so poetic
poetry needs no glue
or so I've been told
by those who know
there is always someone who knows
yes to this, no to that
this is poetry, that is not

when you look at it, not from above
but at a cross section
it is easy to see it
the cardboard
I'm talking about the cardboard
when you look at it closely
you can see it, the waviness

of the centre sheet
attached to sheet A
at the base
and to sheet B
at the top

it is sometimes puzzling
although I don't know why
when you peer through the slice
you'd expect to see
all the way through to the end
but even when you try to
you can't
because of a fold
or because it has been crushed
has collapsed
like my life has collapsed
an irreversible collapse
so said the doctors
with no cure
with no known cure, I would add

corrugated cardboard
is apparently so resistant
that it can take up to one hundred years
for it to disappear

I would be chatting away
keep on talking
and he would tap my knee
with his little hammer

looking through the holes of the corrugation
you can't see a long way
and yet it lasts for a long time
it seems endless
then suddenly it ends

a cardboard box can see a lot of the world
divorces, reconciliations
abandonments by the side of the road
as the garbage trucks make their rounds
on collection day

♦ ♦ ♦

they chose new boxes for me
I can't complain
but from there to say
as I did earlier
that it was out of consideration
I really don't think so
not anymore
I don't know why
I had thought it was
just something that came to mind, I guess

I get the impression I will be changing it frequently
my mind, that is
it is difficult to reason out
difficult to come to a reasonable conclusion
because they threw everything into the boxes
helter-skelter
without bothering about what they were doing
I would have expected them to place my things
in a more orderly fashion
right then and there
I got the impression that this consideration
wasn't consideration at all
it was as if I didn't exist
and yet they were talking to me

they were addressing me when they said:
you won't be needing these anymore
and off it goes! into the box
higgledy-piggledy
there are containers
liquids in bottles
shampoos in tubes
lids that could be loose
it had been a while since I'd bothered to tighten caps
why go to the trouble of closing it all the way when
  you know
that the next morning, you will open it again
to pour some of the creamy liquid into your hands
and rub it through your hair
so what is the point, tell me
of tightly screwing it back on
when the very next day you'll be taking it off
with your hands all wet
your mind half asleep
your eyes half open
and no grip at all

they might all spill out
the liquids can pour out into the box
which will dampen the sides
worse, all could become sticky
the perfume smells will get onto everything
the bars of soap will begin to dissolve

and it will smell like the opera on opening night
I imagine
I've never been to the opera
certainly not on opening night

this is what I call a disaster
if you ask me
medicine
pills dissolving
the plastics might even become
damaged
but no, of course not
what difference does it make
you won't be needing these anymore
so they say
they don't care about the electric razor short-
circuiting
and starting up because the liquids
caused a faulty contact
it will use up the batteries
as well as make the box
a vibrating box
after it has been taped shut
it makes them laugh
their shoes are black like those of customs officers

no reason to open it up just for that
the razor will stop on its own
when its batteries are dead
bzzz, bzzz!
like that, with their mouths
they buzz just for a laugh
as if they were answering the razor
bzzz, bzzz!
my love
as if it were a vibrator *for her*
one in the shape of a penis with rabbit ears
for the clitoris

and the alcohol, did they consider the alcohol?
there is alcohol in everything
in mouthwash, for instance
and that is just one example
the deodorant
the bottle of rubbing alcohol
think about it, for God's sake
rubbing, friction
fire
you have to be careful, you know
and to think you can get boxes with drawers
I've seen them before
like dressers
they could have brought some of those
at least for the bathroom

they could have
but it would have been too costly, I suppose
and so, they threw everything into the boxes
he doesn't need these anymore
higgledy, now you see it
piggledy, now you don't

they were right
it is only after it's gone
that you realize you didn't need it
except, while you have it, it's a must
like in the kitchen
the Black & Decker toaster is a must
the Cuisinart juicer is a must
the Electrolux electric broom's a must for the broom closet
even dust is a must, if you think about it
and Second Cup coffee
and Sunkist oranges
and French bread from Guillaume's Bakery
        on Fairmount
but dust is a special case
no brand name for dust
no trademark
no memorial at the garbage dump
no death notice in the obituaries
for some of us
a pauper's grave will do

you don't need all this dust
of course you don't
they vacuumed everywhere
then they put me into another corner of the room
they vacuumed where I was
where I had been before

one was singing to himself
it's crazy how you see all
hear all
when you are the least bit still
when you stop moving
imagine, I'm just finding this out now
it's not too late
it's never too late, you might say
but it's not too soon, either
I'd rather not talk about it
or say anything
nobody asked my opinion

his partner told him to stop singing
to be quiet, said it was annoying him
as if he was being made fun of
they are so sensitive
in this line of work

the other one stopped gradually
in a decrescendo
as if he were stopping because he wanted to
or had forgotten the tune
or the words
he sang: la-la-la
and finished with a series of pa-pa-pas
like a motor running out of gas
he seemed embarrassed
as for me, I stayed still
said nothing
in solidarity
I didn't sing either

I imagined myself looking down on them
from a hole in the ceiling
into a steam room, a sauna for men
at their manner of approaching
or avoiding each other
their sweat drenched brows
the sweat stains under their arms
awkward glances
avoiding
but avoiding what
the *trade*
at the Montaigne Bathhouse
or at a luxury spa
or a gym locker room

there was a young one among them
he was the one singing
maybe to avoid being hit on

I think he would have been surrounded,
            the younger one
if they had been at a sauna
he was
as they left
he got slaps on the shoulder
his butt was grabbed in a chummy way

like you see the players do during the Grey Cup
a mark of affection, perhaps more
ah well, it isn't for me to say
that's what writers are for

♦ ♦ ♦

others arrived
with boxes that were full
you could tell
I thought that they were going to replenish
what the others had cleared
but no, of course not

I am not used to this type of situation
I'm still gullible
full of delusions
even at my age, even in my state
these ones were dressed differently
blue shirts
cotton trousers
white running shoes
I noticed their hairy arms
it made me think of roustabouts again

but it wasn't as I thought
since it was the contents
of their boxes
that interested them
and these guys had finer builds
they opened the boxes they had brought
after carefully putting them down

the other ones had left with all my things
I knew that I would have trouble getting them back
that wasn't my ambition
I had no more, anyway
ambition, that is

these ones were calmer
the newcomers seemed
more methodical with their boxes
they knew what they were doing
they unfolded the flaps
and voila
the contents were revealed
the boxes stood open
like images of open boxes
or the Dropbox icon on your computer screen
inside there were containers
spray bottles
with a nozzle and gun-like trigger
others with caps
that you can pour from without undoing them
by pulling on a little valve
without even removing the lid
and aerosol cans
and brushes
I was impressed by the brushes
but not as much as I was by the way
everything had been so neatly placed

there was something reassuring about it all
but the boxes weren't clean
there were openings along the sides
openings like wounds
or a woman's shaved vulva
whichever you prefer
I guess you can tell I'm a man
and that I still think of such things
the corners had been ripped
the sides were scraped
with deep grooves
some of the flaps were torn
others had creases
since that is what happens when you close up boxes
by sliding one flap corner beneath another
on all four sides
it works, but at what cost
dog-eared corners
surfaces marred with scars that will never heal
and writing too
on the outer faces
with a fat marker
words encircled
Xs here and there to show which markings
          are to be ignored
traced in haste
crossed out in haste as well
words cancelled
struck out
with different colours

I am repeating myself, you know
how naive I am
and if you didn't know
you must be starting to guess
these guys will replace
what the first ones have taken away
they'll put things on the window sills
bring in little stands
armchairs and end tables
place objects on them
they will redecorate
I will be a new man

but no, of course not
as soon as they opened the boxes
they took out latex gloves
blew air into them
and put them on
rolling the ends up to meet their sleeves
I remember that the gloves were yellow
that struck me
yellow, not yellowed
a beige-yellow colour perhaps
my memory isn't so good
everything is starting to fade
the gloves
yellow, yes
yellowed, no

I'm speaking of this today so that I don't forget
yellow, but not yellowed
pale beige, no doubt
no doubt indeed

they took the containers out
and from the containers they distributed liquids
very deliberately
they put the stuff a little everywhere
some of it was sprayed
liberally, I might add
some they put onto a sponge
after which they started to scrub
with brushes, as well
of different shapes and types
they used J Cloths that they quickly discarded into a
garbage bag
into which they also tossed paper towels
immediately after using them

I watched them go at it
but I got the feeling I was in the way
they would stare at the floor while they worked
or out the window
or at the wall
or else, they stared
at what was at the end of the brush
of the cloth
or the Bon Ami spray

they didn't speak to me
but they talked about me
as if I wasn't there
they would say *this ol' guy*
when referring to me
this ol' guy did this
this ol' guy did that
knick-knack paddywhack!
this ol' guy has been here for ages
this ol' guy had money
or he didn't have much
not so much
on this subject
opinions were divided
they brushed
and they scoured
and they scrubbed
I didn't think it was possible
to scrub so hard
and to have running shoes so white
Adidas
or rather Nikes
since they had that little logo
in the shape of a boomerang

they'll say that I wasn't very concerned
with cleanliness
in the last little while
especially the last little while
let them say what they will
I don't care one bit
I'm above all that

and yet listening to them gossip like that
I felt irritated
it was rude
it was tactless
like the first ones, they didn't bring anything
they were here to take stuff away
but this time
it was the filth that they were interested in
the filth
the stains
the traces left behind, it all amounts to the same thing
the stuff out of your nose
that you wipe on the bed posts
and especially the blood, it's crazy how much you lose
when your back is turned
excrements
they say shit
urine, piss in their vocabulary
the nail clippings had been vacuumed up
by the first team

that didn't stop these ones from finding more
the one with the moustache
I couldn't be sure about the moustache
since he wore a mask over his nose and mouth
as did the others
but I got a sense that there was a moustache behind
          the fabric which quivered
like a membrane
let's say the one with the moustache
I have never sported
a moustache
the one with the moustache said:
don't chance it
pathogens can spread onto everything
he should have said: risk
don't risk it
because here chance doesn't fit
the chance to become ill
the chance to die, you don't say that

the other one looked toward the ceiling
as if he were looking for telltale signs
how could I have got all the way up there?
to that height
in my state
I ask you

he was worried
he was having trouble breathing
I'm sure it was psychological
his anxiety was palpable
it was no doubt the fumes from the chemicals
and it would be a chance now that I think of it
a chance in a million
and that chance, I got it
I'm the winner!

yet I felt fine
if not for this fatigue
I believe I could have said:
I feel fine, doctor
I don't know why I added *doctor*
by habit, I guess
because, everyone knows, that phrase
feeling fine
is naturally followed
almost instinctively
by doctor
you automatically think of health
of not being sick
when you are hospitalized
your life changes
it gets even worse

you couldn't say that I was
ill, really
at that moment in time
maybe before
without a doubt before
an extreme fatigue
shortly before
but who can say that they have never been tired?
there were also fractures
among other possibilities
you can break your ribs
from falling on the stairs
but my kneecap wasn't broken
it responded immediately to the tap of the little
        triangular hammer

I have seen pictures of broken kneecaps
x-rays in black and white
it's not a pretty sight
the bone breaks in two
under the skin
and the pieces move around
it's crazy, you never think about needing one
in order to walk
to kneel down, yes
for that, absolutely!

you need your kneecaps for praying
you also have to join your hands
my little finger wasn't broken
it didn't stick out at an awkward angle
I will say that much
not that anyone has ever asked
I have never been asked if I was a snob, either
when I would hold a teacup
or a glass of water
more and more often a glass of water
because it isn't as hot
there isn't a risk of getting burned
now here, no one would say
a chance of getting
a third degree burn

a glass of water can be tepid
but not tea
tepid tea is not very appealing
I would hold the teacup with both hands
so that I wouldn't drop it
in the beginning, just one hand
then, at the end
I don't know if I held the cup at all
maybe there was a straw
a long straw like a flexible tube
which would soften because the tea was hot
and would close up on its own

I don't think that I was ill
but who can really know?
show me someone who is in stinking good health
and I will show you a breeding ground for germs
blocked arteries
a brain resembling a junior chemistry set
and it will become apparent to you that some
of the contents are missing
that a vial is empty
that the box has been rifled through
that the toxic substances have mixed together
the beneficial ones having already vanished

oh, the little pill bottles
with the child-proof lids
Pantoloc, Crestor, Ativan
with arrows that you have to line up
apply pressure to the top
push down on the cap as you turn it
while keeping the bottom part
from moving
that is what you call
making life complicated
there were some on a table
pills
by the bed
there were
life-complicators

on the shelf
attached to the bed
let's not talk about that
missing was a tray on which to put
Absolute Vodka mixed with orange juice
or flavoured gin and tonic
Beefeater, I would have enjoyed that

I would have fancied myself on a beach
or relaxing by the side of a pool
a Margarita in my hand
there are moments in a life that you yearn for
and others when you would have been better off
somewhere else
moments when you have cried
an arm against a door that won't open
dead ends, impasses
huge ruts in the middle of the road
potholes that cause flat tires
yellow barriers with black stripes
detours signalled by traffic cones
resembling barber poles
but I certainly don't regret the pool
even being half asleep beside it
or the ocean and the waves that wake you up
when you put your chair too close to the water
and the rising tide begins to lick at your feet
sometimes creeping up to your bottom
and in a flash
you wake with a start

♦ ♦ ♦

they took away all my things
but they didn't take my memories
obviously
although
I suppose that they would have tried
if they had thought of it
or else they believed that there was no point
I didn't look like much of anything
anymore

they took everything
you won't be needing these!
what do they know
how can anyone know
what is good for another
what is essential to him
what he can do without
I really wonder
I was trying to stay calm
for once it wasn't very hard to do
I had an infinite amount of patience
I surprised even myself
but all the same!

they left
they took their dirty boxes
into which they had neatly packed
their cleaning products
they had taken off the masks
which restricted their breathing
they seemed like fish in an aquarium
especially the moustached one
their gloves too
not for their breathing
but their skin was affected
their hands were covered in eczema
their skin was blistered
and now they touched everything
without taking precautions
they even felt around in the garbage bag
with bare hands
for some keys that had fallen in
contrary to what you might expect
I wasn't laughing

but they were
they were laughing
they were talking about beer
the one with the moustache said:
I'm dead tired, I need a cold beer!
they laughed even harder
but that one doesn't

the other one said
with his hand in a fist
and his thumb pointing
in my direction
the moustached one answered:
no way, man
on the contrary
it's just what he needs
a nice cold beer to perk him up!
ha! ha!

they closed the door behind them
I could still hear them in the hallway
they were talking loudly
you can work up a thirst
I imagine
doing what they do
but I was left wondering
how can I know
what is essential
what I cannot do without
what does it all amount to?
nothing
my demands had greatly diminished

when I first arrived here
as soon as I entered
I sensed that I would need to scale down

give up a host of big and little things
medium things let's say
like caressing myself
or brushing, it's all the same
blasting my music
grilling steaks on the barbecue
I'm certainly no vegetarian
taking half-hour long baths
until my skin prunes up
and becomes translucent
those kinds of indulgences
you know, life's little pleasures
I had immediately known that it would not do
to cry my heart out
now, I could

I did wonder where I had left my wallet
but it wasn't important anymore
I quickly lost interest in it
the same for my credit cards
my bank cards
and that gold pendant I wore around my neck
I remember that I had offered it
to a woman once
and that she had returned it to me
because she didn't love me
she could have kept it
it's out of the question
really, no!

even scratching myself was out of the question
I love scratching myself
even when I am not itchy
scratching makes you feel alive
first they put mittens on me
then they cut my nails down to the quick
that is why there were clippings on the floor
they had been careless
one team makes a mess
the other cleans up
that's life

you'd think I was complaining
I was complaining, it's true
I never stopped
I criticized
you don't understand
it was my sole occupation
there was a time when I would wake up just for that
and go to sleep telling myself
that I hadn't done enough
that tomorrow would be better
I'd criticize myself
I was concerned about effectiveness
and yet, if I were asked what I regret the most
now, today
I would say: having been too effective
we are never truly effective except against ourselves

every time that something is created
from without
something within begins to perish
there is always something lost
as if we transfer a little part of who we are
to that which we are not

everything comes to an end
sooner or later
that's what she was saying
she just about sang it out
a woman had entered the room
she was wearing white orthopaedic shoes
she worked alone
she had frizzy hair
big-framed glasses
or as you'd say for shoes
big-sized
she, just she
I don't know what else to call her
she used paper towels
a small spray can
it would go pshtttt
a powdery liquid would appear almost instantly
then she would tear off a sheet
straight from the roll
it's filthy, it's crazy how filthy it is in here!
she ranted against the filth

she was very down to earth
she had been attractive
once upon a time
as I had once been, as well
in my younger days

I knew her
she came every day
early in the morning
I never saw her at night
she would always say the same old thing:
so filthy, it needs a good cleaning
Blanche Brightly to the rescue
she was referring to a television ad
I don't believe that was her real name
Miz Blanche
nor even the real name in the ad
imagine that
then I could be Mister Blackhole
since we had never been introduced

she would enter without knocking
there was no latch on the door
so I couldn't have locked it
but a gentle knock-knock
I would have appreciated that
she would burst in with her arm out in front
as if against an invisible entity who was trying to

prevent her
from entering or going any further
she would head straight to the window first
then she would stroll around
indeed, out for a walk in my room

she would come here for a stroll
around where I was
it annoyed me
she'd go about here and there, she unfastened
took something down
she too wanted to take things away
if she had been strong
she would have picked me up
opened the window
and thrown me out
five floors, you could die that way
but she wasn't strong, or not enough
or else she didn't really want to

Saturdays and Sundays
another cleaner, a man, replaced her
the cleaning man replaced the cleaning woman
here, life was simple
but on Mondays she grumbled
she suspected me of being mean-spirited
of trying to be even messier on weekends
of wanting to make her life harder

and yet, and yet
if it weren't for people like me
if it wasn't for me
me, the father of Filth himself
Mister Slob
as she would mutter under her breath
she would have lost her job
and she really needed this job
so she could pay her rent
thank you, O Filth

never would she look at me
I could have not been there
I don't know if she would even have noticed
where the devil has he gone, he has disappeared!
since when do bodies just disappear?

no, not a chance
no more than she had noticed
that the room had been cleaned
from top to bottom this time
that she would be going over it again for nothing
likely she was dirtying more than she was cleaning
that she was smearing the chrome surfaces
and leaving very faint streaks on the windows
which at a certain angle
in the sun
you could see traces of cloth strokes

just as you might see the traces of brush strokes
on paintings of the great masters
the smudge of a rag
on a Renoir
or on the landscape in front of the Notre-Dame Hospital
she was smudging Lafontaine Park

it was none of her business
it's crazy how filthy it is in here
she'd exclaimed every time she entered
Miz Blanche Brightly
a conditioned reflex, to be sure
she scolded as if I had disobeyed her
she asked rhetorical questions
she would throw me a dirty look
on the rare occasions that she deigned to acknowledge
    my presence
as if I was the cause of all the filth
how could it possibly get so filthy!
I said nothing
I played dead
that morning, given the circumstances
it wasn't too difficult, for a change

I never found out who she was married to
she didn't talk about her husband or children
she talked about filthiness
that was her specialty

she knew the entire lexicon
trash, waste, grime, dust
simple words
but also regurgitation, fetid discharge
she knew putrid and putrefaction
mildew and mould
she could tell the difference between the two
words that she no doubt spewed out
day in, day out
because I couldn't imagine
that she adopted this manner
solely for my benefit
perhaps she would carry on at home
her husband would probably look at her
            as if she were mad
he'd observe her while watching
a show on TV
the worst part was during the night
she'd rouse with a start
and get up because there would be a stain on the floor
and she'd go to clean it up
sometimes, she wouldn't wake
she would clean him up, too, in her sleep
with a corner of the bed sheet

♦ ♦ ♦

I'd tell myself that she was my maid
with the emphasis on *my*
she and I, we weren't anything like a couple
a woman, a man

then a real couple came in
one black, the other white
yes, a real couple
a pair, two who were truly alive
and who suited each other well
all the while being very different
that wasn't us
the maid and I
she had left
now it was he and she
a couple had entered my room
he and she
because there was a guy and a girl
the girl was black, the guy, white

and that couple
newly formed
in my view, obviously
newly arrived would be more accurate
had also come to take away
since I've been here, that is all they do
I've been divested of everything

the woman in the couple was black
like the queen in a chess game
she stripped off my clothes
I was in a very peculiar place
that much was clear
she was the one who removed my clothes
it was her job
no doubt carefully worded
in her job description

she pulled off my socks
after having taken off my shoes
needless to say
my shoes were black
then the couple loosened my belt
they worked together
that is when I realized that I was dressed
and that they were a couple
so little ever happens around here
that it all becomes a muddle in the end

the man hadn't come forward until then
so I hadn't given him much thought
in fact, it was the man who unbuckled my belt
slid it out of the belt loops
while the woman took my trousers off
they were very well synchronized
he slapped the belt against her thighs
creating a sharp sound

thwack!
it made her jump
then the woman started to laugh
I thought to myself: oh, for crying out loud
for nothing, because it went no further
she threw him a wink
and unzipped my fly
something was in the way
she had to concentrate
I had an erection
she exclaimed: my word, you don't say!
surely she had seen others
and she giggled
a nervous little laugh
tee-hee!
admiringly, I thought
then she broke it with both her hands
you could hear the *crack*
like when you break a branch
she said: it will be easier this way
he, however, looked somewhat uncomfortable

he loosened the knot
undid the tie
my tie
from around my neck
removed my jacket
raising one arm, and then another

my other arm
I let them do their thing
I still wonder why
so many questions are left unanswered
especially at the end of life

why was I dressed
I want to leave, that is what I kept repeating to myself
I was ready to leave
I would have called a taxi
I would have said: come now, it's urgent!
but how could I
to get a taxi, I would have had to give an address
of where to go
and I didn't have one
I couldn't remember mine
if ever I even had one
no address, no taxi, Mister
Mister who?
Mister Blackhole
is that a joke, or what?
Blackhurst, if you must
Mister Blackhurst

I observed the scene
as if from above
he tried to take my ring off
the fellow

the guy in the couple
if she was the black queen
he would have been the white knight
he worked quickly
while she looked elsewhere
deliberately
I could have sworn to it
I would have known if she had looked at me
he pulled on the finger
and she was still looking away, on purpose
I am sure of it

it wasn't working
my fingers were too swollen
he pulled
it had to be done
quickly
it had to happen effortlessly
smoothly
he took out a tube of some kind of ointment
K-Y jelly
she watched from the corner of her eye
without it seeming obvious
she dusted around the curtain
or wiped the sink
he slathered my finger with the lubricant
he rubbed it
and then tried again
but it still wouldn't come off

the finger remained stiff
swollen around the ring
a wedding band
so, I had been married
until death did us part
my wife and I
he tried to twist the ring off
while using a little push-and-pull motion
nothing was working
it wasn't happening quickly enough
that's for sure!
he let my hand drop
like an embarrassed pickpocket
who replaces it all back into the pocket
ashamed of his clumsiness
his mouth close to his victim's lips
he apologized
to me
I found that strange

the woman said:
we didn't come here to steal
he didn't answer right away
but later, when he did open his mouth
I realized that he was trying to justify himself

that the Earth won't stop turning
for something so trivial
that the world couldn't care less about me,
          or my finger
that it is stupid to leave a gold ring on
to be swallowed up by nature
the opportunity presented itself
it wasn't his fault
he just needed to take a pair of scissors, a scalpel
if she hadn't said: no!
he would have cut off my finger
he would have played with the ring
he would have tossed it into the air
trying to catch it
before it could roll across the floor
and down the stairs

because that is how it was
there was a floor
of white and black tiles
a ceiling
acoustic paneling
four walls of pastel green
they might have played heads or tails
to see who would keep my ring
me, me!
I would have cried out: me!
laughter all around

what's in a ring
can you tell me that?
I could have played
along with them
pretended to be having fun
attempting to get my ring back, as a game
I would have tripped on the woman
I would have kissed her in passing
at first by accident, then on purpose
I would have run my hands through her hair
put my tongue in her mouth
I would have dared
I wouldn't have been scared to

the guy wouldn't have objected
he would have watched
I could tell that he was the watching type
a voyeur
it would have got him excited
he would have enveloped us both
in his strong arms
and would have pressed us together
I would have found this funny
she as well
I would have laughed
I still had courage enough
even in difficult times
and I wondered

whether this time was one of them
like those you hear of, *during difficult times*
and I thought to myself
no
no, finally
this isn't a difficult time

it was even rather easy
in any case, much easier
than I would have imagined
but it was bit of a shock all the same
when another guy
one of those muscular types
with some pliers
went and took down the TV
he said: he won't be watching this anymore
your handsome gentleman
his quip made me feel sick to my stomach
I noticed then that I was dressed
dressed up
in my Sunday best
I suddenly understood what had just happened
there is nothing simple about time
when we are obliged to give a detailed account
my undressing
had happened in reverse
I realized that they had just finished dressing me
and that I had got it mixed up

the sequence of events
everything, all of it
I finally understood
that it had been the other way around
that I had been dressed up and not undressed
that I was ready to go out
I told myself
that I could no longer trust
my own self
and when you can no longer trust yourself
who can you trust?
tell me that
when you no longer have trust in yourself
your judgment
you are better off dead
and it is a slow death
that other one with the pliers
he swore as he worked
I felt a great sense of sadness
no, not in seeing my television go
not in seeing the black queen
and the white knight
pretending to be working hard
in the presence of the technician
for example, pretending to adjust
the knot of my tie
buffing the tips of my shoes to make them shine
freshening me up with a small perfume atomizer

the base of which resembled a flat bottomed bubble
that she held in one hand
while the other hand squeezed the bulb

it made me think of a dance
a threesome, a foursome with me
a choreography
without any particular meaning
other than this, perhaps:
that I had never paid for the television
that there were other bills that would go unpaid
that my reputation had gone out the window
in the eyes of the banks
with my disappearance
my credit rating was in a freefall
God knows, likely my accounts have already been
    closed
my apartment rented out
my belongings put out onto the curb
so much the better!
when I leave, I will be free
I could even change my name
I could call myself Mister Blackhole, no longer
    be Mister Blackhurst
I don't like that name
I have never liked it
I would go to live in another city
in another country

in Argentina, I'd live in Buenos Aires
I would fall in love with *Marta*
I would learn to count in Spanish
uno, dos, tres, cuatro
or in Italian
if ever I decided to go to Italy
instead
they must be similar
one old-world language to another
a different Martha
a different life
a different body even, resembling mine
just as one corpse resembles another

I would have an accent
I would be handsome
because I would be a foreigner
I would no longer have to endure
all the mediocrity
of dying where I was born
I would be in love
and I would no longer have to dress up
like you do for funerals
except on my wedding day

I was inventing all kinds of stories
I knew that I was
I was starting to understand
I had a strange taste in my mouth
metallic
that's when I felt
I really felt that
I was feeling nothing
for the first time
that the time
yes, that the time had come
I remember a phrase
from the Bible
to everything there is a season
and so
when the time comes...
I would have heard that phrase spoken at funerals
but not have understood it
I must admit
so many useless things are said
at such times
things like:
he was a great guy
we're going to miss him

♦ ♦ ♦

people would ask me
how are you doing?
and I would tell them that my health wasn't so bad
a bit sore here, in the throat
an irritation
and my back, and also my rheumatism, I believed
in such platitudes
swollen feet
nobody was listening
gout, perhaps
doctors would look for an excuse to get away
at celebrations and parties
people would say:
there is someone I need to speak with
oh! please excuse me
I must go and say hello to Doctor Kilburn
with the more patient ones, I would start to talk about
      my phobias
my phobia of damaged boxes, you got the picture
boxes with tape on them
marks left from knives, traces where Exactos were used
      to cut them open
I would confide my troubles to them:
yes indeed, you know
to what extent they make my life miserable

I wouldn't elaborate
I sometimes would add: during our moves
they had already moved on
or when I buy cereal
at the store
and the box of Corn Flakes is perforated
by a long cut
oh dear
I'm alone
you just have to put the box
back on the shelf

ah, but
when the time comes
that stayed with me
it's powerful
this phase as well:
to everything there is a season
I guess that I hadn't really understood
that phrase
because of the echo in the church
and the smell of incense that stifled my breath
so I had difficulty *figuring it*
that's how they say it out in the countryside
where I was born
figure it

it kept coming back to my mind
how do you figure out
when the time comes
this phrase
misunderstood, misheard
stayed with me
it had bloomed in my mind
like a flower
ah! such poetry
oh, just a small flower to begin with
plucked from a flower wreath
a flower that I had surreptitiously picked
in the centre aisle of the church
and had placed in my lapel
telling myself
that it was of no use to him
that he didn't need it
the deceased

for me, it was a flower
lifted
for them, it was a ring
to steal
by them, I mean the couple
and the ring
was mine
everyone's life is very similar
them, me, we are all the same
life is the same for everyone
death as well, I assume

I knew what awaited me
when the time will have come
they will arrive with a pump
to extract my blood
and fill my veins with glycol
a chemical compound, a fluid
that they add to windshield washer fluid
so that it doesn't freeze on the glass
so that there's no trace of frost left on it
but I didn't want to think about that
winter is harsh
in this country
I'd rather focus on summer
and glycol
well, that is for when it is cold enough to freeze fire
or for when you are dead

that's what I told myself
it's for when you are dead
they inject the fluid into your veins
that doesn't concern me
so, I just kept quiet
I didn't move
I didn't get offended
when someone exclaimed:
it smells bad in here
or when I saw them enter
as if they owned the place

they were the same ones
they returned full force
the men in black shoes
but were they really the same men?
I don't believe so
there were more of them
three, four, a small group rather than two or three
they were dressed like me or you
well, at least like I was
you, I have no idea
that's not my business

they inspected everything
one even looked outside
through the window
the one that Blanche Brightly had re-cleaned
he didn't notice the streak marks in the sunlight
or he made no remark
about them

they were anxious
not me
they were eager for it to be over with
I made them uneasy
they could only think of getting rid of me
I could sense it
he's not going to talk
the other ones laughed
he wouldn't have talked anyway
yes, but you never know

you never know, it's true
then the one who had gone to the window
suddenly noticed the curtain
he said: what the hell is this?
the answer was so obvious
that nobody answered
they were all stunned
he seemed vexed
he opened the door
and yelled out a name
like Aileen
or Noreen
this could be contaminated!

I already thought a name ending in *een*
was a nice name
perhaps because I only had one other
to compare it with
Blanche, that's also a nice name
but Aileen is prettier
less spic and span
Noreen
would have been too negative
so, Aileen
that's the one I like best
Martha as well
but he had yelled Aileen
and a woman came running

she was spraying an aerosol can
all around me
she said: if I may
they acted as if she had to be tolerated
no one answered her
everything had been taken out
and so, to the one who pointed toward the curtain
she said: oh!

she was young, Aileen
she had a pleasant voice
but he had yelled
and had indicated with his finger
without even stretching out his arm
he simply
bent his elbow
there was something bird-like about his action
not sure which kind
a heron or a swan
I don't know
or a flamingo, very nonchalant
his arm was as pink as a shrimp

she left the room
one of the guys muttered under his breath:
some technician…
the rest, I didn't understand
she came back with a stool

and got up onto it
she lifted her heels
and was on her tippy toes
she had taken off her shoes
I would have liked it if they took mine off
they were pinching my toes
the couple, at least, the man in the couple
the white knight of earlier
had tied my laces too tight
it was very constricting for the feet

Aileen pulled on the curtain
and, when the rod came loose
she toppled to the ground
she had trouble getting up
she had her arms full
no one gave her a hand
even though there were several of them
at least three, maybe a fourth
that I couldn't see
it was a long tulle curtain, nearly transparent
she was rolled up in it
she began to sway
as if she were losing her balance

I could tell that she was dancing
from where I was
I loved her instantly
I danced with her
in my mind
I am like that with love
I waste no time
I would have married her on the spot

she must have understood that I was ready
it was evident from the bulge in my trousers
even broken, I knew that I was responding to her
presence
she danced for me
and, for the first time
since my arrival here
I felt a kind of quiver
but it wasn't very convincing

we don't have only this to do
there are others
stop that
no one repeated that it was unsafe
that it could be contagious
that the germs could have spread to the curtain
in the end, security measures
are tedious

she left
I am sure that the curtain is now in her room
Aileen's room
by her bed
that it sways in the breeze
I can already hear sneezing coming from the building
where she lives
it's coming from her roommate who is having trouble
breathing
those guys don't have hearing as sharp as mine
as for me, I could hear a rock cough in a field
it's just a figure of speech
they went into a fallback position
like in war
like soldiers on the battlefield
on their backs was a kind of apparatus
I hadn't noticed it before
but seeing them back up that way
I couldn't help but notice
they fell back toward the door
in formation
you'd think they were afraid that
I would jump out at them
they exited
I could hear their footsteps in the hall
it was clear that, as far as they were concerned, it was
finished
that they had done enough for me

they had taken everything away
and now, they were taking themselves away
they were leaving
I waited for a short while
not long, not too short either
I allowed for them to go a reasonable distance
I don't know why
it was important for there to be a distance
between them and me
as a precaution, no doubt

I counted to ten
that's easy enough
kind of like the countdown
before a rocket is launched
but I didn't count backwards
from ten down to zero
I found that too complicated

I got up and went to the door
I turned my head around
I looked one last time, behind me
the room was empty
if it weren't for the large box left behind
the room would have been completely bare
the box appeared even longer
viewed from the door
it was a clean box
it was perfect
very symmetric

just slightly wider
where the shoulders go
the lid hung to one side
attached by hinges made of Duct Tape

I realized that they had placed something into it
and that they hadn't really sealed anything
I could have looked inside without any difficulty
I would no doubt have learned a lot
but I told myself
that it would have been an unhealthy curiosity, so
there you have it

I hesitated crossing the threshold of the door
I thought of retracing my steps
to put the cover back on again before leaving
a matter of making everything neat and tidy
less sloppy
but I didn't do it
it seemed senseless
and yet the box was impeccable
just as I like them
my appreciation for boxes
now seemed so frivolous
what on earth had I seen in them?

I had felt a little pang in my heart
for the other boxes
those that contained my belongings
when they had left with them
but now, nothing
I looked at this larger box
made to my measurements, I thought with pride
the most beautiful box
that I had ever seen in my life
and it left me indifferent
I didn't care, I assure you
even if, in pulling the lid back toward me
I would probably have understood something
have read some words, names
dates, even
symbols, perhaps
a cross
and on the top of the box
the lettering done with a marker:
Blackhurst
no Mister this time
just the surname
like for an artist
a Picasso
or a nobody
it's all the same
I didn't care!

I was still standing in the doorway
I told myself:
leave, there is nothing holding you here!
and for once, I listened
I left
but only after
glancing each way down the hall
I could hear the footsteps of the men in black shoes
          echoing in the distance
in the stairwell to the next level, it's possible
in the hall of the ground floor
that too
is possible
the sound of heels against the tiles
guided me
I followed them
at a distance
a safe distance
toward the exit

when I passed through the hospital doors
I saw the parking lot before me
glowing white like a cemetery
I advanced cautiously
there was a blinding sun
the light was unbearable
and the heat
indescribable

it has been three long months
I'm not going to hide it
I'm hungry